The German Social Market Economy
An Option for the Transforming and Developing Countries?

T0346637

THE GERMAN SOCIAL MARKET ECONOMY

An Option for the Transforming and Developing Countries?

DETLEF RADKE

FRANK CASS • LONDON
Published in association with the
German Development Institute, Berlin

First published in 1995 in Great Britain by
FRANK CASS & CO. LTD.
Newbury House, 900 Eastern Avenue,
Ilford, Essex IG2 7HH, England

and in the United States of America by
FRANK CASS
c/o International Specialized Book Services, Inc.
5804 N.E. Hassalo Street
Portland, Oregon 97213-3644

Transferred to Digital Printing 2004

Copyright © 1995 GDI/Frank Cass

British Library Cataloguing in Publication Data

Radke, Detlef
 German Social Market Economy: Option for
 the Transforming and Developing
 Countries? – (GDI Book Series; No.4)
 I. Title II. Series

 ISBN 0-7146-4153-7

Library of Congress Cataloguing-in-Publication Data

A catalog record for this book is available from the Library of Congress.

ISBN 0-7146-4153-7

Contents

Preface

With publications on the Social Market Economy already filling libraries, there has to be a special reason for a further study on the subject. The reason is the political and economic collapse of the socialist states and the subsequent offer from the OECD members to help the new, transforming countries to develop a market economy order. This offer, which has meanwhile assumed practical form with the assignment of numerous "western" advisers to these countries, is based on the implicit assumption that it is clear what constitutes a market economy system. This is, however, seldom the case. In fact, the various OECD countries, as just three of them - the USA, Japan and Germany - demonstrate, have adopted very different types of market economy. It is incorrect, therefore, to speak of *the* market economy system or *the* market-oriented approach. The term "market economy" refers primarily to the abstract principles that regulate and control an economic system; where the practical form of this system is concerned, on the other hand, the term remains equivocal.

This study presents Germany's Social Market Economy. In describing the constituent elements of the German system, it seeks to explain to transforming and developing countries a type of market economy which might be helpful to them as they establish their own market economy models.

The author would like to take this opportunity to thank those with whom he has discussed the subject for the critical suggestions they have made. He is particularly grateful to Germany's Executive Director in the World Bank, Dr Fritz Fischer, for having initiated this project.

Introduction and Summary

The collapse of the socialist states shattered the hope cherished for many decades that development can be planned centrally. The final development decade of this century will therefore be characterized by the efforts of the former Eastern Bloc countries (transforming countries), and of many developing countries, to convert their government-controlled and planned economies into market economy systems.

The transformation of complex systems in what is, as a rule, an extremely unfavourable internal and external environment is one of the most difficult tasks that development economics has ever faced. This applies both to the shaping of processes during the transitional phase and to the definition of the precise goal of transformation, i.e. the market economy model that is to be adopted.

In the debate on transformation problems little attention has so far been paid to the question of the goal of transformation. Interest has instead focused on the problems posed by the practical implementation of reform policies. Given the difficult economic and political situation in the reforming countries, this is understandable. Nevertheless, it is important that the objective of the reforms, i.e. the market economy model actually sought, should be defined at the earlier stage of the transformation process. In the search for an appropriate market economy model the transforming and developing countries can and should consider the experience of the industrialized countries, which have adopted many variants of the market economy.

This study presents the economic system of the Federal Republic of Germany, the *Social Market Economy*. The aim is to describe the elements of this system which ensure its openness, dynamism, efficiency, stability and social balance. Of particular interest in this context are the elements that distinguish the German system from other market economy systems. The study thus seeks to identify what is specifically German about its market economy system rather than to explain how a market economy system works, taking Germany as an example.

As will be shown in the various sections of the study, the Social Market Economy is anything but a perfect system. It has many weaknesses, outmoded features and signs of fatigue and fails in many respects to fulfil the hopes pinned on it. It also remains to be seen whether it will meet the challenges of the future as convincingly as those of the past. If the Social Market Economy is nonetheless singled out from the many variants of the market economy that actually exist as a possible option for transforming and developing countries, then mainly for two reasons.

Firstly, it has proved to be a very successful economic system in the past forty years. Long regarded as an "economic miracle" after the end of the Second World War, the German economy has for many years occupied a leading position among the highly developed industrialized countries. The success of the Social Market Economy is particularly evident when the yardstick used is not only the annual growth of the gross national product but also such values as social justice, the humanization of the workplace, the democratization of the economy and the protection of the environment.

Secondly, the Social Market Economy differs significantly from the market economy systems of other industrialized countries. This is particularly true of the market economy models in the Anglo-Saxon world and Japan. Germany's Social Market Economy also differs from the other market economies of continental Europe, although the differences are not so pronounced now as they were in the 1950s and 1960s. With the advance of Western European integration, it can even be predicted that the further development of the Social Market Economy will occur in the context of the European Union.

To describe the profile and constituent elements of the Social Market Economy, critical detachment is needed. This study is not therefore the place for a detailed critical analysis of the form the German system actually takes. Many of the issues being hotly debated in Germany today are, moreover, of little or no relevance to the transforming and developing countries. They include the considerable financial burden that the completion of German unity is imposing on the old Federal Republic, the threat to the social system posed by the increasingly unfavourable age structure of the population and the desire to continue occupying a leading technological position. The transformation of the former East German economy is again so specific a case that it cannot serve as a model to the other transforming and developing countries.

Germany's Social Market Economy is the outcome of an evolutionary process in which economic, cultural, political and historical factors have had as much impact as the political decision-makers' desire to shape the economic system. It is primarily due to the particular situation facing Germany after the Second World War that conceptual ideas initially had a decisive influence on the West German economic system.

The concept of the Social Market Economy is based on the view that, as none of the various spheres of man's life exists in isolation, they have to be shaped in accordance with uniform principles. This "unity of the style of formal social principles" is to be achieved on the basis of political liberalism. Democracy and market economy are seen as a single entity.

It is government's task to create and sustain an environment that enables the individual to develop his economic capabilities to the full. A functioning competitive order is therefore regarded as the crucial basis of the Social Market Economy and as one of the main tasks of government economic policy; other economic policies must be guided by the principle of competition.

Government's second major task is to ensure that economic processes are socially balanced. In the Social Market Economy, therefore, market forces are restricted by numerous rules and regulations concerning, in particular, free collective bargaining, the protection of labour, democratization of the economy achieved through a very wide-ranging Labour-Management Relations Act and a social security system based on the principles of the social state, solidarity and subsidiarity.

Favourable internal and foreign policy environments in which the German economy was able to develop after the Second World War have also made a decisive contribution to the success of the Social Market Economy. Particular emphasis must also be placed on German society's system of values, in which economic success occupies a very important, though recently declining, place, and on the determination of the political decision-makers to keep the economy and society "open", i.e. to expose them to constant pressure to adjust. It is primarily due to cooperative federalism, an essential feature of Germany's federal system, that it has been possible to raise living standards to roughly the same level throughout the country. No other major industrialized country has so regionally balanced a structure in terms of economic strength and living conditions. The broad institutional infrastructure, the dual system of vocational training and the monetary and financial system, which is characterized by an independent central bank pursuing the goal of price stability and by all-purpose credit institutions, have also made a major contribution to the strength of the German economy.

In the final section the study asks how far the Social Market Economy can be regarded as an option for transforming and developing countries. It concludes that the Social Market Economy is of interest to this group of countries in two respects. On the one hand, it provides a number of partial solutions, such as cooperative federalism, the dual system of vocational training and the monetary system, which can at least serve as a model for reforms undertaken in these spheres. Above all, however, the Social Market Economy reveals that, in addition to the various, sometimes technical arrangements, there are fundamental principles with which an economic system must be aligned. Here the Social Market Economy stands for a type of economic order with which the attempt is being made to harmonize individual freedom, economic efficiency, social justice and the protection of the natural resources on which man depends.

1   Conceptual Foundations

After the end of the Second World War Germany faced the task, unique in its history, of creating a new economic order, an order which not only broke with the National Socialist war economy but also took account of the negative experience of the Weimar Republic and especially the disastrous effects of hyperinflation and the world economic crisis. This explains why conceptual ideas had a far greater influence on the economic system of the Federal Republic of Germany than on the economic systems of other countries.

The concept of the Social Market Economy has its roots in the ordoliberalism established by the Freiburg school.[1] Ordoliberalism is based on the realization that none of man's various spheres of life exists in isolation: they are closely linked. It follows from this interdependence that subsystems must be shaped in accordance with uniform criteria. This "unity of style" is to be achieved on the normative foundations of political liberalism. The freedom of the individual must be preserved in all spheres of human existence against the background of natural economic scarcities and the conflicts inherent in any society.

The concept of the Social Market Economy can be seen as a comprehensive attempt to shape the economic sphere and thus of the social system in line with this unity of style. Neither a capitalist market economy nor a centrally administered economy is capable of this since both are unable to safeguard, or even explicitly proscribe, the civil rights and liberties of the individual. The Social Market Economy, on the other hand, is a synthesis of liberalism and socialism with which the relationship between competition and solidarity, between market economy and social balance is redefined. It can also be defined, therefore, as an order that seeks to combine the individual's free enterprise with social progress on the basis of the competitive economy.

An efficient competitive order is the crucial element of the Social Market Economy. Establishing and preserving this order is one of the most important and comprehensive tasks to be performed by government economic policy. Performance-based competition is encouraged as the economic basis of social security and social progress and also accepted in principle as the regulator of income distribution. However, to contain the disparities that would occur in society if market forces were given a completely free rein, government is assigned the task of pursuing an active social policy. Those who are unable to participate in performance-based competition and do not therefore earn a market income are not only to be assured of survival but also to participate in economic progress.

Government economic policy is thus essentially *Ordnungspolitik*, i.e. a policy geared to the establishment and preservation of an order which gives the individual the greatest possible freedom and is economically efficient and socially just. Since the 1980s this *Ordnungspolitik* has been extended to include the protection of the natural environment. It is not for government, on the other hand, to pursue active structural, industrial and technology policies, especially if they restrict the independence of individual enterprises in their decision-making. Nor does the formulation of binding national technology or foreign trade objectives and strategies have a place in the concept of the Social Market Economy, even if they were to be the outcome of a dialogue between government and the business community.

Over the past 40 years the concept of the Social Market Economy has not been fully implemented. In a pluralist society, with its numerous particularist interests, it is evidently not possible to gain more than limited acceptance for a consistent economic policy geared to the overall system. Furthermore, the political parties have themselves encouraged developments that run counter to the Social Market Economy model. The individual's freedom of action has been increasingly restricted, for example, by a constantly growing flood of laws and regulations, and government social policy has largely supplanted the individual's responsibility for his own welfare.

Presenting the Social Market Economy as a concept of an economic order that has sound theoretical foundations is not therefore without its problems. For this reason the Social Market Economy will not be described in the following in terms of this concept. Instead, the study singles out those factors which can be assumed to have contributed to the success of the Social Market Economy, whether or not they form part of the concept.

2   The Social Market Economy as Part of the General Order: Political, Normative and Historical Background

Stability of the internal and foreign policy environments

Germany's Social Market Economy is integrated into its political system, parliamentary democracy. The economic and political subsystems have been linked in the past forty years to good effect. The high level of internal acceptance of parliamentary democracy has helped the Social Market Economy to develop in an extremely stable political environment. Conversely, the economic successes of the Social Market Economy have enhanced the acceptance of the political system.

No less important a requirement for the development of the Social Market Economy was a stable foreign policy environment. With Germany's historical balance of power policy abandoned in favour of unequivocal orientation towards the West, the post-war period saw the establishment of an external policy framework that was reflected in the Federal Republic's commitment to the European Community and NATO. From this framework its political and economic system has received a significant, fortifying impetus.

For Germany the positive links between the internal and foreign policy environments on the one hand and economic development on the other are so self-evident that they do not require further explanation here. Various elements of the political system and the effect they have had on the economic system will be discussed later.

Primacy of economic values

Economic successes and peak performances occur whenever people are prepared to subordinate everything to their economic interests. This is as true of individuals as it is of groups and societies. It is probably immaterial whether it happens because of external pressure or voluntarily.

Historically, it has been predominantly the societies of Europe that have developed an economic and work culture that manifests itself in the recognition of the economic potential in everything and in the use of everything to preserve and develop the material basis of life. This "mercantilist propensity of the European mind" was due to the unprecedented unleashing of productive forces and improvement of material living standards.[2] And it is this propensity that distinguishes the European from other advanced civilizations.

Today it is not only European societies that subscribe to the primacy of economic values. Besides the USA, various Asian countries in particular have devoted themselves almost unconditionally to a policy of growth. It is difficult to say why certain societies are prepared to subordinate all important spheres of life to the cause of economic success and attempt to become economically superior to other nations. All that seems certain is that this willingness does not stem from the way in which the economic system is organized, from the peculiarities of the political system or from a particularly favourable natural resource endowment, although natural resources may encourage or obstruct the full development of all productive forces.

In Europe the countries that were particularly active economically lay mainly in the west and middle of the continent. The countries to the north and south and certainly to the east usually had other priorities.[3] Although the economic sphere was not despised in these regions, it was never rated as highly as in, say, Germany. *"In these regions intact social networks, relations and neighbours, for example, were (and are) far more important than mere economic success. Having or making time to enjoy creative leisure or even doing nothing at all, in short being economically unproductive, was (and is) - to varying degrees - the expression of a life worth living rather than reprehensible idleness."*[4] The "economic content" of the relationship that society and the economic order enter into may thus vary. In the economic statistics it is reflected in higher or lower productivity figures. Even if every country in the world adopted a market economy system, there would still be a sizeable prosperity gap.

This background reveals the true significance of the adjectives used in other countries to describe Germany's economic and work culture - industrious, diligent, punctual, disciplined, etc. What is meant is a basic human aptitude, which is evidently more pronounced in German society than in many others, an aptitude to make economic success the most important yardstick of life.

Germany's economic success in the past forty years can be ascribed primarily to the strong desire of its people to build a new society from the ruins of the Second World War. If the people had not been prepared to work hard, the German "economic miracle" would not have been possible and Germany would not have been able to remain one of the major industrialized countries.

Even basic human aptitudes change with the passage of time. Just as a society's will to perform well economically can grow, developments may occur that qualify the importance of the economic sphere. In Germany such developments have been discernible for some time. With prosperity increasing at an unprecedented rate, there are signs, as one generation gives way to the next, of a change of values, which will have a momentous impact on future economic development. In general, this change of values is reflected in a downgrading of economic goals. The economy and the environment are largely seen as forming a single entity today, as the call for a socially and ecologically compatible market economy shows. Similarly, there has been a shift in the relative importance of leisure and work. Fewer hours a year are now worked in Germany than anywhere else in the world.[5] Attitudes to work and health have also changed. Among the OECD countries, Germany is second only to Sweden in terms of absenteeism due to illness.[6] This can be partly attributed to abuse of the dense network of social security provisions. More important, however, is how well Germans believe they have to be to go to work. While absenteeism because of a slight cold, for example, is socially acceptable today, only a far more serious affliction would have kept a man from his workplace twenty years ago.

As a social objective, economic growth has now lost its overriding importance and its ability to achieve a national consensus. As the differentiation of German society increases, the objective function has become more complex and also less certain. The ability and willingness to adapt have declined appreciably in favour of protecting of the status quo. With growing frequency the flexibility of the economic system is restricted by barriers newly erected by the change in the system of social values.

Historic opportunity for a fresh start

After the Second World War West Germany had a far better opportunity to make a completely fresh start than any other industrialized country. Post-war Germany's political elite were aware of their historic task. They succeeded in designing a new political and social order, making West Germany a modern democratic industrial nation. At a stroke, it was able to rid itself of past aberrations, ossified structures and many antiquated customs. In many sectors of the economy and society the institutions, organizational structures, coordination and control procedures that emerged were more efficient than those of other industrialized countries.

Two decisions taken at this time should be singled out: firstly, the decision on the Basic Law, which sets out West Germany's political constitution; secondly, the decision to adopt the Social Market Economy as the economic system to which the country is committed. With these two decisions the two abstract principles, democracy and market economy, assumed their specifically German form. Their distinctive features will be considered in the following sections.

One of the peculiarities of post-war Germany was that its policy was subject to Allied approval. In their efforts to prevent the re-emergence of a strong centralized German state the Allies established a political framework for Germany's reorganization. The new West German state was to be federal, with a weak central authority (Federal Government) and strong *Länder* (States) and municipalities. This led to the creation of the *Bundesrat* (Council of the States), an institution which gave the *Länder* a powerful right to participate in the shaping of the country, and of a fiscal system in which the functions and revenue of the three levels of government were constitutionally defined. The central authority was also to be denied direct access to the central bank. This eventually resulted in the passing of the *Bundesbank* Act, which ensures that the *Deutsche Bundesbank* is largely independent of the government. On instructions from the Allies the large industrial cartels were also broken up, thus laying the foundations for an effective competitive order. In other words, Allied requirements played a not inconsiderable part in paving the way for decentralized and federal solutions in West Germany, solutions which can be seen as a model for many countries today.

West Germany's political front-line position is another of the peculiarities that have consistently influenced German economic policy in the past forty years. Owing to its geographical position West Germany more than any other western industrialized country found its system laid open to comparison with others, and this meant above all successfully standing up to the competition in the social field. It may be precisely because of the East-West conflict that the ambitious concept of the Social Market Economy was abandoned in favour of a welfare state, in which governments can demonstrate their concern for social justice "day in, day out".

3 Openness of the System

If development is regarded as an open, spontaneous, indeterminate and unpredictable process, the only societies with a chance of holding their own in this process are those which cope with constant change by being open rather than shutting themselves off and inventing all manner of taboos. A system in which there is no place for the unpredictable will be brought down by the changes around it. Market economies are open systems; they represent a framework that permits societies to react "productively" to problems, desires and challenges. However, the degree of openness that market economies actually demonstrate not only differs from one country to another but also varies appreciably over time.

The success of the Social Market Economy is not least due to the fact that it has always been more open in its external relations than most other forms of market economy. None of the major industrialized nations has integrated itself into the international division of labour as resolutely as Germany. Where trade policy is concerned, Germany is a proponent of liberal world trade, although its options are limited within the EU framework. All administrative restrictions on international capital movements and direct investment were removed long ago. When internal economic problems arise, Germany has always been willing to undertake structural adjustment. Mention need only be made in this context of the structural adjustment processes in the textile, shipbuilding, coal and steel industries in the post-war period.

An economic system does not become open automatically: openness has to be created by a workable competitive order and a strict competition policy. Without competition economic systems lose their openness and so cease to be innovative and dynamic. They are pressured and overwhelmed by every innovation for which they themselves have not initiated. It is hardly surprising, therefore, that the German *Competition Act* is known as the Basic Law of the Social Market Economy. This reflects the overriding importance attached to the competitive order and competition policy in the Social Market Economy.[7]

The most important instruments defined in the *Competition Act* are the prohibition of cartels, the control of mergers and the control of abusive practices by market-dominating enterprises. The prohibition of cartels is designed to prevent enterprises from reaching agreements that restrict competition (agreements on prices, quantities and regional market shares). The control of mergers enables the amalgamation of enterprises to be forbidden where it would result in a market-dominating position or strengthen such a position. The aim of the control of abusive practices is to protect small competitors against obstruction and exploitation by market-dominating enterprises. A separate supervisory authority, the Federal Cartel Agency, was set up to enforce the *Competition Act*. It enjoys virtual judicial autonomy and is independent of the Federal Government, particularly in the decisions it takes in individual cases.[8] Enterprises must also comply with the *Prohibition of Unfair Competition Act*, which requires market operators to observe the "bonos mores" that have emerged in the economy and have been accepted by the legal and business community as fair and just.[9]

As in most countries, certain sectors of the German economy are not or only partly subject to competition.[10] All in all, however, the permissible restrictions of competition are the exception rather than the rule. The German economy is left very largely to fend for itself in national, European and international competition. The extensive process of concentration that has occurred in the German economy is not inconsistent with the high degree of competition. As a rule, the Federal Cartel Agency has permitted enterprises to merge provided that the pressure of competition has been maintained by foreign companies.[11]

The German economy has also been open in sectors more closely related to social policy. It has thus come to terms, albeit reluctantly in many cases, with the obligations that ownership of property entails, with a wide-ranging law on employee participation and comprehensive social systems and with the extension of the concept of the Social Market Economy to include the ecological dimension. For their part, the trade unions have abandoned the ideology of the class struggle and adopted a sectorally oriented wage policy that reveals a sense of responsibility to the national economy.

Openness entails not only the opportunity to decide one's own future but also the risk of failing. In an open system everything is in a state of flux and must be constantly questioned, adjusted or even abandoned. Market economy systems are therefore in permanent conflict with the nature of man, with his indolence, his fear of risks, his demand for security and clear prospects. Keeping systems open is consequently a political feat since it requires of the political decision-makers that they block the easy way for society and commit it to behaviour patterns that call for a high degree of willingness to adjust on the part of the individual citizen (and voter) and often lead to success only in the longer term.

Whether Germany's Social Market Economy will continue to show a greater degree of openness than the other major market economies in the future is uncertain. The many instances of ossification and paralysis which the German system has experienced over the years cannot be overlooked. A growing amount of social energy is no longer converted into kinetic energy but dissipated in internal friction. German society is scarcely capable of fundamental reforms today - not, at least, when the political and economic situation is normal. The fact that such tendencies are also to be observed in other democracies should be no reason for complacency. There are many signs that openness, flexibility and willingness to be innovative will count for more in the future than they do today. We are experiencing an expansion of the world economy, requiring more structural change of us, and an acceleration of advances in knowledge, causing many things to age more quickly. Competition is becoming more dynamic.[12]

4   Federal Structures

After the Second World War the victorious western powers insisted that the Parliamentary Council they had commissioned to establish the Federal Republic of Germany organize West Germany along federal lines. This led to the creation of a democratic, social federal state with a territorial division that departed significantly from the boundaries of the traditional *Länder*.[13] One advantage of the largely arbitrary restructuring of West German territory was that most of the resulting *Länder* were economically viable and a reversion to "federal particularism" was avoided.

The first peculiarity of Germany's federalism is the form taken by its political decision-making. This includes the constitutional position of the *Bundesrat*, the body representing the *Länder* in the legislative process: all laws affecting the interests of the *Länder* require the approval of the *Bundesrat*. Of perhaps even greater importance for everyday policy-making is the complex political interplay of the federal, *Land* and municipal authorities. This form of interaction, also known as cooperative federalism, is both vertical (from federal to *Land*,

Land to municipal level) and horizontal (between *Länder* and, to some extent, municipalities).[14]

German federalism is based on the constitutional provisions relating to public finance. They govern the vertical and horizontal distribution of tax revenue among the Federal Government, *Länder* and municipalities commensurate with the tasks required of them by the constitution and with their economic capacity. Revenue is also apportioned horizontally among the *Länder* and vertically (in the form of supplementary payments by the Federal Government) to improve the financial strength of the poorer *Länder*.

In the case of horizontal revenue apportionment, the wealthier *Länder* make compensatory payments to the poorer *Länder*. The first step in this form of revenue apportionment is to determine the financial strength of the various *Länder*, i.e. their total revenue (including that of the municipalities). The financial strength of a *Land* is then compared with its financial requirements, which are calculated by multiplying the national average of per capita revenue of all the *Länder* by the number of inhabitants in the *Land* concerned. *Länder* whose financial strength exceeds their financial requirements must make contributions to less fortunately placed *Länder*. The aim of horizontal revenue apportionment is to raise each *Land* to at least 95% of the average financial strength of all the *Länder*. Guarantee clauses ensure that no *Land* required to make compensatory payments falls below 100% of the average per capita revenue of all the *Länder*.[15]

Supplementary payments by the Federal Government (vertical revenue apportionment) complement horizontal apportionment. These payments are non-specific allocations from the Federal Government to economically weak *Länder*. Total supplementary payments of this kind are currently limited to 2% of value added tax revenue.

Municipal self-government is another feature of German federalism. It has a long tradition in Germany. It focuses on

- the provision of public technical services (water, electricity and gas supply, refuse collection, street lighting),

- the provision of cultural and educational facilities (schools, training centres, libraries, theatres, museums, etc.),

- the financing of social activities (nursery schools, old people's homes, hospitals, sport, social welfare, youth services) and

- municipal building (road and housing construction, urban and transport planning).

For these activities of direct local interest the municipalities are entitled to their own revenue, which they may also use as they see fit.

The rights, obligations, functions and revenue of the Federal Government, *Länder* and municipalities have been continually reviewed and adjusted to new conditions in a complicated and on-going political process. Despite incessant criticism of details, it is generally agreed that the cooperative federalism that has emerged in Germany as a reasonable compromise between centralism and federal particularism.

The interplay of political federalism and Social Market Economy has had a decisive influence on economic development in Germany. In market economies there is an inherent tendency for regional imbalances and agglomerations to emerge. Centralized countries are inclined to exacerbate these imbalances to the advantage of their political capitals. The general failure of these tendencies to take root in Germany is largely due to its federal structure. The overriding aim of German federalism, which is enshrined in the Basic Law,[16] is uniformity of living conditions throughout the country. The achievement of this aim in political practice has resulted in the supply of public goods - from roads and training centres to cultural institutions - being roughly the same in all the *Länder*. None of the larger western industrialized countries has so balanced a regional structure in terms of economic strength and living conditions as Germany. This is primarily due to the interaction of market economy and federalism.

Germany's federal structure has also led to an unusual feature not to be found, or not to the same extent, in other industrialized countries: competition among the various *Länder* for the most successful policy of attracting industry. No *Land* government can afford to fall too far behind the other *Länder* for too long. It would constantly have to account to its own voters and to the more successful *Länder* required to make compensatory payments.[17]

5   Institutional Infrastructure

Germany has a dense institutional infrastructure covering and permeating all aspects of life.[18] This network of government, parastatal and private institutions gives the country's economic and social system structure and stability. Obvious though the positive correlation between institutional infrastructure and economic development is, it is difficult to prove in terms of strict causality.[19] Above all, it is impossible to identify a given institutional structure as being the best for development processes. The tasks, political and constitutional background, past patterns of development and options and other environmental factors are too diverse to permit a country's institutions to be assessed on the basis of economic criteria.[20]

No attempt will therefore be made in the following reflections to identify the particular features or profile of Germany's institutional infrastructure. Instead, they will focus on two aspects: the effectiveness and the efficiency of public institutions, with effectiveness meaning what they are expected to achieve and efficiency referring to the input needed if they are to live up to this expectation.

Effectiveness

Public institutions are expected to provide services that nature, scale, quality and timing of which meet the needs of society. Measured against these four criteria, Germany's public institutions must be regarded as being, on the whole, highly effective.

Nature of services: The public institutional infrastructure in Germany has become so dense over the past four decades that in principle it covers all areas in which society expects public services to be provided. In this respect it does not have any shortcomings. In fact, the opposite can be assumed; that at least is the inference to be drawn from the intensive debate on the privatization of public utilities that has been going on for some years.

Scale of services: Understandably, a lack rather than an excess of public services leads to criticism. They may be lacking if the institutions concerned are not efficient enough; but, as a rule, the fault lies in a shortage of financial resources and staff. In such cases, it is not the institutions but the political decision-makers or the priorities they set that must be held responsible for poor public services. Major deficiencies in public services are to be found primarily in certain areas of the social policy, a sphere in which the Federal Republic has already achieved very high standards.[21]

Quality: The quality of the services provided by the public institutions can be regarded as generally high. In particular, the many institutions in the areas of measurement, testing and quality control and the various economic monitoring and supervisory agencies enjoy a reputation of being very reliable, correct and professional. Where they have discretionary powers, their decisions are based on objective criteria geared primarily to the interests of the public as a whole rather than specific groups.

This positive assessment also applies, by and large, to the competence of the political administration and of public institutions that have to take decisions in highly politicized fields, i.e. the government departments at federal and *Land* level and a number of public-law federal institutions or federal agencies (the Federal Cartel Agency, the *Bundesbank*, etc.). Criticism of the work of these institutions is due in most cases not to their inadequate effectiveness but to the lack of political support for the decisions they take.

Timing: Effectiveness also means providing services at the appropriate time. With some, though important, exceptions, the German institutions can certainly be said to satisfy this criterion. In the areas where decision-making takes too long it is not, as a rule, the institutions that are to blame but the political environment in which they operate. This will be considered at greater length in a moment.

The considerable expertise, reliability and correctness of Germany's public institutions can be attributed to various factors. For one thing, their staff are highly professional, not least because of the extensive training opportunities offered by the public service. Good technical equipment also augments the professional competence of institutions needing modern technical devices to do their work. The correctness of the public institutions can probably be ascribed to relatively good working conditions and to the self-image of the German civil service of being committed, as servants of the state, to the public interest. Though they also occur in Germany, corruption scandals are comparatively rare.

The assessment of the effectiveness of the public institutions would be incomplete without a reference to the increasingly long and expensive authorization procedures governing private and public investment. Although no accurate statistics on this aspect are available, there are many indications that the authorization of any investment relating to actual or potential environmental pollution and/or public health risks takes years. Germany probably has longer authorization procedures today than most other countries. This development is due to the growing fragmentation of the overall order, changes in the system of social values and a mounting volume of legislation.

With the creation of a parliamentary democracy after the Second World War, the German administration faced what was probably the greatest challenge in its history. It had long been accustomed to wide discretionary powers, which it wielded "at arm's length" from society, although this did not necessarily mean it did not know how to use these powers for the good of the general public in many cases.[22] Now it must account for everything it does, to a public, for example, that articulates its views through the mass media, to those directly affected by the action it takes and to the political leadership (parliament and government). Increasingly, it must have the legality of its measures and decisions reviewed by administrative courts. It must take appropriate decisions in a permanent "dialogue" with well organized interest groups that are in close contact with the political leadership.

In these circumstances, an administration is obviously less eager to take decisions, acts more cautiously and is itself instrumental in reducing its own discretionary powers by initiating legislation and drawing up detailed implementing regulations. The administration's effectiveness is thus threatened not from within, through, say, the departure of qualified staff for the private sector, growing corruption or declining skill levels, but primarily by a changing social environment. In many areas the German administration is now barely capable of discovering what is in the public interest, by which it is supposed to be guided, or of asserting itself when faced with well organized interest groups and politicians guided by the majority view. Its actions are increasingly determined by political opportunism and risk minimization, accompanied by the prolongation of decision-making processes.

Another factor which reduces the effectiveness of the public institutions, but for which they similarly cannot be blamed, is the increasing volume of legislation. The constantly growing stream of laws and regulations, domestic and European, is steadily outstripping the administration's processing and implementation capacity. On the one hand, its need for internal coordination is growing; on the other, the consistency of the provisions to be implemented declines as the volume of legislation increases. In other words, the administration is left to implement conflicting provisions. It is increasingly confronted, after all, with laws and regulations with built-in derogations. Although this approach makes it easier for compromises to be reached at political level, it shifts the responsibility for problem-solving to the level of the administration, which is left to decide how to deal with these derogations.

Efficiency

The assertion that, on the whole, the public institutions operate effectively is not inconsistent with the criticism voiced by the public that there is too much bureaucracy and sloppiness in the public sector. The public institutions are accused of being too slow, too labour-intensive and so too expensive. The reasons for poor efficiency are numerous. They include:

- the impossibility of dismissing public servants,

- the promotion of staff on the basis of seniority and party membership rather than performance and

- the absence of incentives for good performance and of penalties for misconduct and incorrect decisions.

All public institutions are, moreover, monopolies, i.e. "protected" against competition at all times. Nor do they need to draw up balance sheets and are therefore "spared" the adjustment processes that are commonplace in the private sector.

In these circumstances, it would be unrealistic to expect of the public institutions a level of efficiency comparable to that of the private sector. All past attempts at a sweeping reform of the public administration and other areas of the public sector have failed before they really started. Rarely in the more than forty years of the Federal Republic's history have public institutions been abolished. Adjustment to society's changing demand for public services usually takes the form of the expansion of existing institutions or the establishment of new ones, internal reorganization being a rarity. In efficiency terms the public administration is undeniably one of the areas of German society that is incapable, or virtually incapable, of reform. One solution would therefore be privatization, an appropriate alternative in at least some areas of the public service. Here again, however, it must be said that the *Länder* and municipalities in particular have so far made little effort to seize the opportunities that privatization offers.

To complete the picture, it should be added that throughout the public sector there are segments which operate extremely efficiently. It should also be emphasized that the generally low level of efficiency is often due to bureaucratic procedures rather than a lack of commitment on the part of the staff. And finally, the administration has repeatedly proved that in an emergency, especially when under considerable public pressure, it is capable of mobilizing enormous reserves. The completion of the Treaty on German Unity within a matter of months is an example of how efficient the public administration can be.

Relationship between effectiveness and efficiency

If pronounced effectiveness and generally poor efficiency are features of Germany's public institutions, the question is how this relationship should be assessed with regard to the process of economic development. Once again, it is impossible to produce any hard evidence. There is, however, much to be said for the argument that the effectiveness of institutions is far more important in the development process than their efficiency, provided that the latter does not fall below a certain level.

For the process of economic development it is particularly important for a society to have such institutions as the Federal Cartel Agency, the Federal Banking Supervisory Agency, the Federal Debt Administration, the Federal Materials Testing Agency and the Federal Statistics Agency, which perform the tasks assigned to them correctly and in the public interest. If these services are provided at rather too much expense, scarce resources are admittedly wasted, but in terms of long-term economic development processes this tends to be insignificant.

An example may illustrate this: the German *Bundesbank* is held in high regard for its monetary policy; its professional competence is undisputed. Yet, with almost 18,000 employees, it is over- rather than understaffed. Compared with the benefit which the German economy derives from the stable and internationally recognized *Deutsche Mark*, the untapped productivity reserves of the *Bundesbank* are a negligible factor. Much the same can probably be said of the relationship between the effectiveness and efficiency of most other public institutions.

6   Education System

The efficiency of an economy very much depends on the skills of its people. Germany has an internationally high standard as a location in this respect. It is based on an efficient education system.

From the economic angle, the education system has the important task of teaching the skills which economic development requires. Technical progress and a growing international division of labour cause technical requirements not only to change constantly but also to become far more stringent. Germany attempts to meet this challenge by giving young people a broad and sound basic education.

To only a very limited extent is the knowledge taught in general schools directly applicable to working life. They focus on the general education and the comprehensive development of the personality of their pupils.[23]

One factor that makes Germany particularly attractive as an industrial location is its dual system of initial vocational training, which is complemented by numerous specialized vocational schools, academies, etc. No other country has a training system that is comparable in form and content.

The dual training system is characterized by the combination of practical training in a firm or inter-company training centre and theoretical instruction at a (part-time) vocational school, usually for 8 to 10 hours on one or two days of the week.[24] The vocational schools also have the task of enhancing the general education of their pupils, taking particular account of their vocational aptitude. About 60% of the instruction in vocational schools is technical, 40% general. The aim of the dual system of vocational training is to give young people a broad basic training followed by gradual specialization. It is also intended as the basis for continuing training, which enables the individual to adjust to technical, economic and social development and to advance in his chosen occupation.

Initial training is currently provided in 450 officially recognized occupations, for which uniform minimum requirements have been defined in each case. The employers, trade unions and government are involved in the development of the training regulations and ensure that firms and vocational schools comply with them. Compared with other forms of vocational training, especially that provided by full-time vocational schools, training in a firm and a vocational school is the most popular option. At present, 70% of young people are trained in this way.

For the business community the dual training system is expensive. In 1990 it spent DM 83 billion, equivalent to 3.2% of the gross national product, on initial and in-service continuing training.

Since the Second World War the German universities have been unable to regain the reputation they once enjoyed in the world as centres of research and learning. The relationship between society and the

universities has long been seriously strained; the gap between them
has grown too wide. Research has largely moved from the universities to scientific institutes, large research establishments and private
companies. Nor are the universities wholly proficient in the performance of their educational function. Quantity takes precedence over
quality: there are too many students studying for too long, and what
they study does not adequately meet practical requirements. A comprehensive reform of the German universities is overdue.

Another aspect of the German system is the continuing training which
enables employees to obtain additional qualifications. While the continuing training systems of many other countries largely perform the
functions of initial training, Germany's is geared far more closely to
the continuing training that rapid technological change demands.
Most of this training is provided by the private sector.

Finally, there are retraining schemes, which are financed from unemployment insurance contributions and are intended to improve the
prospects for workers made redundant by technical progress of taking
up a new occupation after additional training. The rise in unemployment in the 1980s led to a substantial increase in retraining measures.

7   Monetary and Financial System

The *Deutsche Mark* is among the world's stablest and strongest currencies; it is the monetary anchor of the European Monetary System.
Its international strength can be attributed to two factors in particular:
first, the major importance attached to the goal of monetary stability
in Germany; second, the institutional mechanisms created in the
1950s to ensure that this goal would always be achieved.

The broad social consensus on monetary stability is closely linked to
the Germans' past experience of inflation and currency depreciation.

In the early 1920s large sections of the population lost all their savings as a result of unprecedented hyperinflation; the currency reform of 1948 showed the German people once again that their money and all financial assets denominated in *Reichsmark* were worthless. In these circumstances, the stability of the new *Deutsche Mark* clearly had to be made the monetary policy's most important gauge. Although this historical experience may have been supplanted to some extent by the current experience of the advantages of relative monetary stability, the fear of inflation and currency depreciation is ever-present in the minds of the German people.

The *Deutsche Bundesbank* was made the country's supreme monetary institution. Under the *Bundesbank* Act it bears sole responsibility for the stability of the *Deutsche Mark*. It is independent in its pursuit of this goal, i.e. it is not bound by instructions from the government. It is merely required to support the Federal Government's general economic policy while performing its task. No other central bank in the world has so strong a formal position vis-à-vis its government.

The independence of the *Deutsche Bundesbank*, which is enshrined in law, is reinforced by two other provisions: it may grant the Federal Government and the *Länder* only short-term loans within narrow limits defined by law. This put a stop to any thought of financing public budget deficits with central bank loans, as had happened on a grand scale after 1914 with the dropping of the gold standard. Furthermore, appointments to the two highest decision-making bodies of the *Bundesbank* - the Central Bank Council and the Board of Directors - are made on the basis of so balanced a formula and for so long a term (eight years) that it is virtually impossible for the government to influence central bank policy.

It would be a mistake to infer from the German example that only independent central banks can ensure a high degree of price stability. An international cross-section comparison shows that central banks bound by government instructions can be very successful in combating inflation.[25] However, these (few) countries attach much the same

political importance to the stability of their currencies as Germany
does. The question of a central bank's independence therefore appears
to be of secondary importance if a government is determined to de-
fend the stability of its currency. The decisive question, however, is
how long governments - especially in parliamentary democracies - are
politically capable of continuing to pursue this objective. The fact that
most western industrialized countries have far higher rates of inflation
than Germany indicates that a country would be well advised to build
a high "wall" around the central bank's printing press so as to contain
the "covetousness" of state and society.

The other striking feature of the German monetary and financial
structure is the universal banking system. In no other country has the
universal bank assumed so distinct a form. Unlike the banking system
common in the Anglo-Saxon world and Japan, where banks confine
their activities largely to deposit and credit business, while shares,
bonds and the like are handled by firms specializing in securities,
German banks offer a complete range of financial services. The "all-
round financial business" they have been conducting for some years
even includes services which have traditionally been provided by the
insurance industry. Many universal banks also have their own economic advisory and real estate companies to back up their credit business.

Compared with other banking systems, universal banking has certain
advantages and disadvantages. The advantages lie mainly at microe-
conomic level in the shape of risk and cost advantages for the banks.
Universal banks are also more resistant to cyclical fluctuations and
changes in their clients' investment behaviour. Consequently, no
other country has as many banks with prime credit rating. The universal banking system similarly has a number of advantages for
clients. They largely consist in a better range of services provided by
a dense network of branches. However, there are also conflicts of interest, one being due to the banks' preference for meeting the private
sector's capital requirements by lending rather than issuing securities
(shares, industrial bonds). As a result, the stock market in Germany -

compared to other countries that do not have a universal banking system - has less width and depth. Although the size of the domestic capital market is not in itself an economically important criterion, it is undoubtedly a disadvantage in allocation terms for private-sector borrowing to be almost entirely confined to the banking system.

The real objections to the universal banking system stem from another consideration: the fear of an excessive concentration of economic power. Indeed, no other branch of the economy in Germany has so much influence as the banking sector. The banks' position of power is only partly based on their many holdings in enterprises, their presence on the supervisory boards of most joint stock companies and their right to vote clients' deposited shares at company meetings. This problem is primarily due to the close, long-term relations between individual firms and "their" banks. The fact that the banks have become "house banks" is a specifically German development that dates back to the early days of industrialization. It is a position that gives them an almost unrestricted insight into the efficiency, strategic planning and investment projects of their clients. In return, however, the latter expect their banks to give them the financial leeway they need to carry out their planned investments.

From the angle of *Ordnungspolitik* such links between banking and private-sector interests may be difficult to justify. However, the advantages of this close relationship should not be underestimated. Firms are not, for example, abandoned when confronted with the financial constraints that economically difficult times bring. Major crises in the past have shown time and again that the banks are prepared to commit large sums of money to ailing clients, though only under public pressure in some cases. A further advantage of close, long-term relations with banks, which has become evident only in recent years, may well be that the managers of German enterprises are able to concentrate on their real tasks rather than devoting much of their energy - as in countries that do not have a universal banking system - to warding off actual or suspected take-over bids.

The main task for *Ordnungspolitik* is thus to recognize the dangers inherent in the abuse of the German universal banking system and not to gloss them over. Here again, the most important means of nipping such abuses in the bud is effective competition. Otherwise, it is for the banks themselves to decide how they use the power they derive from the universal banking system. As long as they behave with a sense of macroeconomic responsibility, as they have in the past, there is no reason to make fundamental adjustments to the German universal banking system.

8 Organization of the Labour Market: Free Collective Bargaining and Labour Market Policy

Free collective bargaining and an active government labour market policy have a decisive influence on the German labour market. These two phrases stand for a set of rules and regulations by which the "free play of forces" in the labour market is rendered largely ineffective. The justification given for this is that, as there is a fundamental imbalance between supply and demand in this market, precautions need to be taken to protect the individual supplier of labour.[26] In addition, the German labour market has been influenced - to a greater extent than all other commodity and factor markets - by historical developments that foiled unrestricted liberalism in labour relations. The main factors to be borne in mind in this context are the German workers' movement, the Catholic social doctrine, the inflation and world economic crisis of the 1920s and 1930s and the competition from the planned economy systems in the post-war period.

Free collective bargaining

Free collective bargaining has rightly been called the "Magna Carta" of the German employment system. It is characterized by two basic ideas: first, employees are to be put in a position to safeguard their interests collectively vis-à-vis employers: second, pricing in the labour market is to remain free from government influence.

The collective representation of interests for the purpose of safeguarding and improving working and economic conditions presupposes the right of association. This right is granted by Article 9 of the Basic Law. The autonomy of the two sides of industry is guaranteed by the Collective Agreements Act. Although it could be amended by a simple parliamentary majority, this Act has a de facto constitutional quality.[27] The state is required to remain impartial in collective bargaining.[28] The judgments of the labour courts are of considerable importance for the manner in which collective bargaining is conducted. Some aspects, such as the right to take industrial action, are based entirely on case law, other aspects, like protection against dismissal, social plan benefits and employee pension schemes, to a significant extent.

Wage negotiations take place at two levels; a distinction therefore needs to be made between sectoral wage policy and corporate wage policy. **Sectoral wage policy** concerns:

-   **outline wage agreements,** defining for several years (usually three) the general principles governing remuneration, e.g. the differentiations of jobs by the qualifications needed;

-   **wage and salary agreements,** specifying the terms governing remuneration, i.e. the level and nature of increases in income, for a period of nine to eighteen months;

-   **skeleton collective agreements,** the outcome of negotiations on the general working conditions that are reflected in non-wage labour costs. They cover, for example, working hours, leave, the continued payment of remuneration in the event of illness, capital-forming payments, agreements on short time, rules on protection against dismissal and agreements safeguarding employees against the consequences of rationalization.

Employees' collective interests are represented by seventeen sectoral
trade unions, which all belong to the Federation of German Trade
Unions[29] and are politically independent. They are faced by 46 industrial associations, similarly with sectoral affiliations. The prelude
to the annual wage negotiations is formed by "wage guide rounds" in
a number of selected sectors of the economy. Although the collective
agreements concluded in these cases are not binding on the other
unions and industrial associations, they set the scene for the negotiations in the other sectors.[30] As a whole, this procedure gives rise to a
wage policy that differs only slightly from one sector and region to
another. The separate development of sectoral factor remunerations
due to different trends in sectoral productivity is a gradual and
lengthy process in Germany.

Not all wage negotiations come to a successful conclusion immediately. Industrial action in the form of strikes and lock-outs is, however, regarded by the unions and employers' associations as a last resort. It is preceded by a complex arbitration procedure. This too is
the responsibility of the two sides of industry. Government merely
has the right to offer its services as an impartial mediator in difficult
conflicts. Until the arbitration procedure has failed totally, both sides
are under an obligation to refrain from taking industrial action.

Collective agreements are regarded as minimum agreements. They
may be supplemented or bettered in corporate wage negotiations and
by voluntary payments by employers.

Corporate wage policy is pursued within the limits of employee participation in corporate decision-making defined in the Labour-
Management Relations Act. This permits the works council, the body
representing the interests of the employees, and the management of
the company to reach internal agreements. Works councils are not
trade union bodies, but independent councils representing the employees of a plant in accordance with the Labour-Management
Relations Act. Corporate wage policy focuses on corporate social
benefits and the rights of the workforce to a say in the introduction of

new technologies and working methods. Corporate agreements cannot supersede current collective agreements.

The most important unilateral **voluntary corporate benefits** are supplements to collectively agreed wages. They are often seen as making the relatively rigid system of collective agreements more flexible or as a move towards factor prices determined by the market. Experience does not, however, confirm this view. Sectoral wage increments rise at roughly the same rate as collectively agreed wages. German employers have rarely taken advantage of the possibility of reducing voluntary payments to compensate for the wage increases forced through by the unions (ratchet effect).

Government labour market policy

The two most important areas of government labour market policy are legislation on the protection of labour and labour market policy in the narrower sense, which has full employment as its goal.

Over the years legislation on the protection of labour has given the employee almost total legal protection against health hazards at the workplace and the social consequences of illness. Germany's employment law has thus largely become social welfare law. The most important areas governed by this legislation are:

-   labour protection in the narrower sense: accident prevention, health protection and rules on when and how long employees may work,

-   the continued payment of wages, leave and protection against dismissal,

-   the protection of certain groups of employees: pregnant women and young mothers, young people, home workers and the seriously disabled.

An important role is played by the decisions of the labour courts, which have done a great deal to interpret and develop these statutory provisions. Since the 1980s there has been a tendency for labour protection to be extended to include protection against unjustified dismissal and severance arrangements.

The second task of government labour market policy stems from the call for full employment. In practical terms, its aim is to increase the individual's employment prospects by improving the transparency of the labour market and occupational and regional mobility. A wide range of instruments has been developed for this purpose. They include placement and career guidance services and measures to promote training and mobility. Provided certain requirements are met, employers can also obtain funds to preserve jobs at risk and to create new ones.

Where employees lose their jobs or their employer becomes insolvent, they receive unemployment benefit or are paid their net earnings for a set period before bankruptcy proceedings begin. Unemployment benefit averages two thirds of the net income last earned. The period of entitlement depends on how long the applicant was employed and on his age. The lower limit is 156 working days, the maximum 832 days.[31]

Conclusion

The labour market is the area in which the differences between a market economy organized in accordance with neoliberal principles and a Social Market Economy are most clearly revealed. It is not the price mechanism that determines the level of factor remunerations and thus the level of employment but trade unions, employers' associations and government, each with their own political and social objectives. Although the main actors are committed to economic rationality, it is not their only yardstick.

Free collective bargaining is based on a broad social consensus. It makes for virtual equality among the parties to agreements, the struggle over income distribution is governed by an appropriate procedure, and the parties to agreements have dealt with each other reasonably. Germany loses fewer days to strikes than any other Western European country.

The labour market policy has reached a stage where further expansion does not seem wise. For one thing, the differences between employment and unemployment are tending towards zero; for another, it seems questionable whether the increased use of traditional labour market policy instruments can significantly reduce the high level of structural unemployment that emerged in the 1980s despite a high rate of economic growth.

In the context of growing unemployment increasing reference has been made in recent years to the pronounced inflexibility of the German labour market, the limited degree of labour market policy differentiation and the high level of wages and non-wage labour costs. These three factors do indeed indicate the need for a critical review of the German system.

Free collective bargaining and the government labour market policy have made the German labour market too weak and too ponderous in its response to a worsening economic environment and competitive position and to technological changes. The obstacles include not only factor remunerations but also the rules on working hours, which prevent, for example, both the time over which German capital stock is used (machine running times) from being increased and retail outlets from opening at times that suit consumers.

Collective agreements in particular fail to differentiate sufficiently in the areas of "vocational qualifications" and the "productivity" of the various sectors and firms. This is due both to the nature of collective agreements, which always tend to eliminate differences, and to competition among the trade unions, which does not allow any of them to

fall behind the general trend in wage agreements. The main aim of
the unions in wage negotiations is, after all, to protect the interests of
their own members. As most union members belong to the lower and
middle wage groups, poorly qualified and even unskilled workers are
comparatively well paid in Germany. The downward differentiation
of wages is thus blocked.

While the limited flexibility and inadequate differentiation in the
German labour market have been deliberately tolerated in the past on
the grounds that they make for social peace and a general social consensus among the relevant groups in society, the current debate indicates that far greater importance is now attached to the criteria of
flexibility and differentiation as means of safeguarding Germany as a
location for economic activity.

For employers the legislation on labour protection means above all
higher non-wage labour costs. It has played a major part in making
labour costs higher in Germany than anywhere else. Although such
statements need to be placed and interpreted in a wider context, it is
still true to say that, as social arrangements do not come free, the effect that any increase in social security has on the competitiveness of
the economy should be constantly reviewed.

9   Democratization of the Economy

Co-determination has a long tradition in Germany. Having been primarily geared in the nineteenth century and first half of the twentieth
to an improvement in the legal and economic position of the employee
at the workplace, it was extended in the Social Market Economy to
become a comprehensive system of democratizing economic activity.
The German system of co-determination is essentially based on the
"non-capital forms" of participation, i.e. participation by wage
labour. Co-determination rights arising from employees' capital hold-

ings in an enterprise are of secondary importance. German legislation on co-determination makes a distinction between employee participation in plants and employee participation in enterprises as a whole.[32]

Employee participation in plants is compulsory in any plant in Germany that normally employs at least five permanent workers entitled to vote. Under the Labour-Management Relations Act employees have the right to participate in corporate decisions through the works council elected by them, and particularly

- a mandatory right to participate (a right of veto or approval) in decision-making on social matters,

- graded rights to participate in decision-making on personnel matters (appointments, dismissals),

- the right to be informed, to be consulted and to be involved in decision-making on the plant's economic affairs.

Employee participation in enterprises is restricted to joint stock companies, except in the iron, steel and coal industries. It consists in the institutionalized participation of employees' representatives in supervisory boards and thus in management's decisions on corporate objectives and measures likely to lead to their achievement. This form of participation enables employees to ensure that their interests are taken into account in any corporate concepts that are adopted; it also makes employees jointly responsible for corporate policy.

The extent of employee participation depends on the size of joint stock companies. In joint stock companies with a workforce of up to 2,000 the employees' representatives make up a third of the supervisory board. In all larger joint stock companies there is parity of employer and employee representation on supervisory boards, although management has the last word since the chairman has a casting vote.

Employee participation in the iron, steel and coal industries goes a step further in the case of joint stock and limited liability companies.

This employee participation model, which owes its existence to conditions imposed by the Allies, takes the last word away from management. Employees and shareholders appoint the same number of members to the supervisory board. They are joined by an impartial member, on whom the two sides must agree.

The relevant legislation has raised the rights of German employees to participate in corporate decision-making to a level which leaves little room for further improvement without changing the very foundations of the Social Market Economy. If employee participation were to be further increased, liability and decision-making authority would be split, i.e. management would have to answer for decisions taken by the employees' representatives.[33] A distinction needs to be made between the formal legal rules on employee participation and their practical application in plants and enterprises. What should not be overlooked in this context is that in many cases both employers and employees still have mental reservations about cooperating as partners.

10 Social Security System

The Federal Republic's social security system is based on the principles of a social state, solidarity and subsidiarity. The principle of the social state stems from Article 20 of the Basic Law: "*The Federal Republic of Germany is a democratic and social federal state.*" This principle entitles the legislature

- to compensate for social differences and so to ensure social justice and

- to attain and maintain social security for the citizen.[34]

The social state does not seek to care for and look after the citizen in every way. On the contrary, solidarity and subsidiarity also require the individual citizen to act socially in solidarity with others and especially to resort to individual and collective self-help and to render social assistance. The principle of subsidiarity even places the individual and the family at the centre of the social system. Action by the state is appropriate only when it is unavoidable. *"If the individual is unable to help himself, he should be assisted ... first by his family, the neighbourhood, a self-help group and voluntary welfare services and lastly by state institutions."*[35]

A distinctive feature of the German social system is the organizational variety of insurers. There is no single insurer, but instead a wide range of public insurers, self-governing institutions and non-profit associations. The state merely prescribes general conditions for the activities of the various insurers. In social insurance, for example, the insured and the employers can manage their own affairs through their representative assemblies and management boards. The insured hold "social elections" to decide which candidates or social groupings are to safeguard their interests in the assembly.

The social security system rests on the following three pillars:

-    **social insurance,** comprising pension, health, accident and unemployment insurance,

-    **welfare and compensating payments,** especially child, housing and education allowances and payments to certain groups of disabled people and

-    **supplementary welfare services** in the form of youth services, health care and social assistance.

The most important of these three forms of services is social insurance. It is organized in accordance with the insurance principle. The insured pay contributions, which entitles them to benefits - based on the individual amounts contributed in the case of pension and unemployment insurance and on the criterion of the collective provision of necessary medical services in the case of health insurance. Where welfare and compensating payments and supplementary welfare services are concerned, the emphasis is on need and social justice.

Pension insurance

Everyone employed for remuneration is required by law to contribute to a pension insurance fund. However, income is considered only up to a given level, which is set anew each year to reflect the general trend in incomes. In 1993 this "income threshold" was DM 7,800 gross per month. Income above this threshold is not considered in the calculation of insurance contributions and has no influence on the level of the later pension. Self-employed people have the right to join the statutory pension insurance scheme.

Pensions are financed by the "pay-as-you-go procedure", the funds being obtained equally from the employees' and employers' contributions. If contributions do not cover current pension payments, the Federal Government is under an obligation to make up the difference. The most important feature of the statutory pension insurance scheme is the index-linking introduced in 1958, i.e. the annual adjustment of pensions to the general trend in wages. This is intended not only to maintain average living standards after a lifetime of work but also to enable pensioners to benefit from improvements in productivity and the current growth of incomes.

The statutory pension insurance scheme is intended to meet basic needs. As a rule, pensions are roughly sufficient to maintain living standards in old age. After 45 years of insurance contributions the net pension amounts to 70% of the earned income last received. Statutory pensions are increasingly supplemented by company pensions and private life insurance.

Health insurance

The statutory health insurance scheme is compulsory for all employees up to a given income threshold, which is set anew each year.[36] Employees and employers pay equal contributions, the Federal Institute of Labour paying the contributions of the unemployed. Contributions that have to be made from pensions are divided equally between the pension insurance fund and the pensioner. The insurance cover is comprehensive, i.e. it extends to all medical care, including early detection, and there is no time limit.

Where ill health prevents an employee from working, he remains on full pay for six weeks. The health insurance companies then pay sickness benefit for up to 78 weeks within a three-year period.[37] The role of private health insurance companies is largely confined to people who are not subject to the statutory insurance obligation, i.e. higher income earners and the self-employed. They too have the right to join the statutory health insurance companies. Slightly more than 90% of the German population belong to the statutory health insurance scheme, while 8% are privately insured. The proportion of those who are not insured has steadily dwindled and now amounts to only 0.3% of the population.[38]

Allowances and compensating payments

Allowances and compensating payments, which are financed from tax revenue, are intended to help achieve certain social objectives or social justice. The most important welfare allowances are child, education and housing allowances. Compensating payments are made to population groups who have suffered injustice as a result of war, persecution or acts of violence.

Supplementary welfare

Supplementary welfare is a comprehensive, non-contributory system of social assistance for emergencies with which the individual is unable to cope on his own. Supplementary welfare benefits take second place to other national social insurance and welfare benefits; they act as a "safety net below the safety net" of the higher security systems of social insurance and welfare. The scale and nature of the assistance provided, which may take the form of personal help, money or non-cash benefits, always depend on the individual case. In the vast majority of cases the person requesting assistance is legally entitled to it. Foreigners in possession of a permit giving them the right to reside in the Federal Republic are similarly legally entitled to maintenance, health care and supplementary welfare benefits.

A special feature of supplementary welfare is the interaction of public and voluntary services. The latter are provided by voluntary organizations and societies that have set themselves the task on ideological or humanitarian grounds of helping people in need and, to this end, have established numerous institutions, such as hospitals, social centres and advice bureaux. Supplementary welfare services, including those provided by voluntary bodies, are largely financed from tax revenue.

Weaknesses and dangers

The social security system has made a major contribution to the achievement of the goal of social justice. In their interaction social insurance, allowances and supplementary welfare produce a safety net of social security that protects all population groups against the serious risks of life. Rather more than 30% of the gross national product has been spent on this system in recent years.

Like all other social sectors, the social security system needs to be constantly reviewed for undesirable developments and necessary adjustments. One undesirable development that has been apparent in the system for many years is the growing importance of the principle of the social state at the expense of solidarity and subsidiarity. While the contention that the social security system is based on these three formal principles may describe the intentions of the leading political parties, it does not reflect reality in the 1990s.

The contest among the political parties for the voter's favour has led to a substantial increase in the citizen's legal entitlement to social services in the past. The individual's responsibility to provide for himself is limited to taking out supplementary private insurance if need be. Relatives are now enlisted to support their dependants only in a "socially compatible form"; the main burden is borne by the insurance industry. Solidarity is being steadily reduced to government-decreed solidarity. As, however, there is no mutual social monitoring in large collectives of the services used by their members, as there is in small groups, the tendency to try to get as much out of the system as paid in is growing. The thoughtless and even abusive demands on the system make this de facto decline of solidarity abundantly clear.

The principle of the social state, subsidiarity and solidarity are no longer in balance. After forty years of government social policy the relationship among them needs to be redefined to place greater emphasis on subsidiarity and solidarity. This is unlikely to be initiated from the political arena for the time being, since none of the parties would want to be accused of dismantling the social security system. Nonetheless, they will be forced to take drastic measures in the relatively near future, since the social security system has already reached its financial limits. Given the extremely unfavourable demographic trend in Germany, not only the scale of benefits but also the distribution of burdens will have to be thoroughly reconsidered. And this reorientation is likely to lead to far less emphasis being placed on the principle of the social state and greater importance again being attached to the individual's responsibility to fend for himself.[39]

11 The Relevance of the German Model to Transforming and Developing Countries

The interdependence of its various subsystems is the main obstacle to the transfer of a given type of market economy to other countries. This is true both of the "model country" and of the "transforming country", and the problem arises for both the economic system as a whole and its individual parts. In other words, a country's economic system with all its ramifications is inseparably linked to the general social system and receives crucial - positive and negative - stimuli from it. Free collective bargaining in the labour market, for example, presupposes the political right of association, the dual system of vocational training requires a business community that is prepared to accept the social responsibility of training young people, and the independence of the *Bundesbank* is guaranteed only if the executive and legislature are willing to relinquish a substantial portion of the power they might otherwise wield over economic policy.

There is no such thing as an economic system divested of its social links. The Social Market Economy is to be had only with its non-economic environment. There is consequently no lack of references to the fact that a market economy is attainable only within the framework of a democratic social order. As long as only the German model is meant, this statement is correct. The democratic cooperative federal state is an integral part of Germany's Social Market Economy. The statement becomes problematical, however, when democracy is generally postulated as a requirement for market economy systems.

When the discussion turns to the abstract principle of a market economy rather than a given real type, it ceases to be possible to forge a close link between market economy and democracy. The terms "market economy" and "democracy" stand for concepts that are not accurately defined. In reality very different forms of market economy and democracy are to be found, and there are numerous possible combinations. The success of certain Asian countries proves that liberal economic systems are also compatible with authoritarian political systems. China and Vietnam will show whether market economies are also a viable long-term option for communist regimes. At least these two countries are already proving that what are in western eyes completely opposite formal principles can be applied for a transitional period, the alternative to dictatorship often being not democracy but chaos.

The transfer of real market economies with their entire non-economic environment to transforming and developing countries is an unrealistic idea if only because it would require the recipient countries to abandon their national identity. Never in the history of civilization has the culture of one country been imitated by another systematically and consistently in its original form.[40] The combination of a country's own social substance and the new regulative market economy principles will always give rise to something new, which can be neither the German Social Market Economy nor another real type. *"Wherever regulative market economy principles ... are combined with societies that have evolved over the centuries, new qualities, strengths and weaknesses emerge."*[41] The alchemy of society and economic order may give rise to very dynamic economies, as a number of Asian developing countries have proved. Whether this experience can claim to be valid for all transforming and developing countries is likely to be questionable. Important though the conversion of their economies to market economy structures is, it is no guarantee that the pending economic and political problems will be successfully solved.[42]

The development of a new economic system is one area in which the transforming and developing countries must go their own way and, in what is bound to be a lengthy search, find the market economy order they consider best suited to themselves. They do not need to reinvent the wheel in the process. They can and should examine the elements and principles that give existing market economies and also social systems their "individual" style. At the beginning of the transformation process the question of a country's own market economy model may not yet be given priority; the pressure of the problems that need

to be solved immediately is too great. But the longer the reform process continues, the more urgent the question of a market economy
model becomes. A reform policy that sees the establishment of a market economy primarily as a technocratic problem runs the danger of
being confronted with developments that were politically unintended
and have to be corrected later. Conversely, a guide to the system to
be adopted facilitates decision-making in individual cases, a process
in which a wide range of options should always be considered.

The debate on the Social Market Economy should therefore initially
serve solely to draw attention to the formal principles underlying the
German economic system. As has been stated in the previous chap-
ters, many of these principles were derived from ordoliberalism.
Some emerged only in the course of economic and social development, partly at complete variance with the doctrines of ordoliberalism. The main style elements and formal principles that characterize
the overall system are:

- **The relationship between the political and economic systems:**
  democracy and the Social Market Economy are seen as a single
  entity. The freedom of the individual is indivisible; it cannot be
  restricted to the political sphere: it must also be achieved in economic activity. This entails, for example, the right to the private
  ownership of means of production, the freedom to undertake independent economic activities, freedom of contract and the right
  to choose one's occupation. Closely linked to this is

- **The democratization of economic activity:** the idea of the ma-
  ture and free citizen finding fulfilment in everyday political life
  by participating in political activities is matched in economic life
  by participation in economic activities through his right as an
  employee to be involved in his firm's decision-making.

- **The relationship between central and decentralized structures:**
  the Social Market Economy stands for cooperative federalism,
  i.e. a middle course between a unitary state and particularism.
  This federal structure is guaranteed by a fiscal system whereby
  the lower territorial authorities in particular are entitled to raise

the revenue they need to perform the tasks assigned to them by the constitution. In principle, decisions are to be taken at the level closest to the citizen (principle of subsidiarity).

- **The degree of openness of a society:** the Social Market Economy is characterized by a competitive system and competition policy that demand a high degree of internal and external openness. The goal is dynamic and efficient competition. A special institution, the Federal Cartel Agency, ensures that the rules of the market economy are observed.

- **The social commitment of private property:** without questioning the principle of the ownership of means of production, the social commitment of private property requires that its use comply with many social norms.

- **The social arrangement of the economic system** is intended to ensure that no one is prevented by his state of health or by professional factors from undertaking a gainful activity. Those who are unable to work have a right to a decent existence; a decline into poverty and deprivation is incompatible with the goals of the Social Market Economy.

The following formal principles relating to parts of the overall system should be emphasized:

- **The dual system of vocational training,** as an alternative to full-time training in school and to on-the-job training.

- **The monetary and financial system,** with a central bank that is not bound by instructions from governments and universal banks that have largely assumed the role of "house banks" in their relationship with enterprises.

- **A labour market** in which the price mechanism has been largely abandoned in favour of collective wage agreements to protect the structurally weaker actor and in which free collective bargaining leaves no room for government intervention.

- **A social security system** which - building on the principles of the social state, solidarity and subsidiarity - compensates for social differences in society and ensures the social security of each individual citizen by means of a comprehensive system of social services.

Whether the way in which these formal criteria have been applied in Germany is relevant to the developing and transforming countries is for them to decide. Nothing would be more disastrous than to want to impose the German (or any other market economy) model on them. As market mechanisms can only be put into operation in a given form, never in the abstract, there is, however, a real danger of ideology being exported with the advice on economic policy given to transforming and developing countries.[43]

The industrialized countries with market economies should confine themselves to describing and explaining their own economic system to the transforming and developing countries, particularly with regard to its normative foundations and its links with the overall social system. A study comparing the formal principles and style elements of the most important market economies might therefore prove very informative for the transforming and developing countries. In the final analysis, however, these countries must have the right to choose from the variants of existing market economies the formal principles and style elements they consider appropriate to themselves.

Notes

1   H.J. Thieme, *Soziale Marktwirtschaft*, Bochum 1990, p. 10.

2   See M. Miegel, "Alchemie des Reichtums", in: *Die Zeit*, 4 May 1990, pp. 41 f.

3   Ibid.

4   Ibid.

5   In 1992 industrial workers governed by collective agreements worked 1,665 hours in West Germany compared to 1,771 hours in France, 1,912 in the USA and 2,040 in Japan. Cf. *Informationsdienst des Instituts der deutschen Wirtschaft*, Vol. 19, 3 June 1993, p. 3. On the other hand, German employees not governed by collective agreements, i.e. middle and higher management, work extremely long hours.

6   Time lost due to illness, health cures, maternity leave, etc. in 1992 amounted to 208 hours per industrial worker in Sweden and 146 in (West) Germany, compared to 33 hours in Japan and 55 in the USA. *Informationsdienst des Instituts der deutschen Wirtschaft*, op. cit.

7   The future of the German competition policy is increasingly influenced by the European Union, although it remains to be seen how successful the Federal Government is in persuading the more defensive members of the EU to accept its offensive concept of competition.

8   The decisions of the Federal Cartel Agency may be reviewed by the appropriate courts. The Minister for Economic Affairs may also overrule decisions taken by the Agency and permit mergers if the resulting restriction of competition is balanced by macroeconomic benefits or the merger is justified by an overriding public interest. The cases in which the Minister has hitherto authorized mergers in this way have been few, but significant.

9   The *Prohibition of Unfair Competition Act* forbids, for example, ruinous price-cutting, slander and libel affecting creditworthiness, the disclosure of commercial secrets and misleading advertising.

10 Agriculture, transport, coal, steel, the public utilities and housing being the main ones.

11 The Monopolies Commission, which since 1974 has been required to report to the German *Bundestag* at two-yearly intervals on the concentration of enterprises in the economy and on the activities of the Federal Cartel Office, also states that the trend in concentration gives no cause for concern. See also E. Kantzenbach, "Wettbewerbspolitik in der Bundesrepublik", in:

K. Fasbender / M. Holthus / E. Thiel (eds), *Elemente der Sozialen Markt-wirtschaft*, Hamburg 1991, p. 256.

12 See H. Giersch, "Wenn Größe zum Fluch wird", in: *Wirtschaftswoche*, Vol. 20, 14 May 1993, p. 25.

13 Only Bavaria and the Hanseatic cities can look back on a period of uninterrupted territorial continuity.

14 Cooperation between the Federal Government and the *Länder* is ensured by some four hundred standing committees. The Financial Planning, Business Cycle, Scientific and German Education Councils have become coordinating bodies of a special type and importance. Cooperation among the *Länder* is no less close. Particular reference should be made in this context to the Conferences of the Prime Ministers and Ministers and the many committees and commissions they have formed.

15 German unification has undermined this procedure. The old system worked because per capita tax revenue in the (old) *Länder* did not differ appreciably and compensatory payments were not therefore excessive. But unification has opened up a wide East-West gap, which cannot be closed by compensatory payments or would overextend the old *Länder* politically and economically.

16 See Articles 72 and 106 of the Basic Law.

17 Some *Länder* have, however, succeeded in keeping pace only at the expense of above-average indebtedness. But federalism is less to blame for this defect than the fact that the new *Land* boundaries drawn after the Second World War were not always appropriate from the economic viewpoint.

18 The term "institution" refers to organizational units and not - as it is increasingly used in the literature - to socially recognized rules of appropriate behaviour in interpersonal and repetitive decision-making processes, i.e. institutionalized forms of behaviour.

19 How much influence institutions have on a country's development is revealed by a comparison with countries whose institutional infrastructure is inadequate. It is not without reason that development cooperation with developing countries, for example, is increasingly focused on the promotion of institutions.

20 G. Püttner, *Verwaltungslehre*, Munich 1989, p. 64.

21 Examples are the shortage of cheap housing in the cities and bottlenecks in social care for people on the poverty line, the number of whom rose sharply in the 1980s. Since 1970 the number of recipients of social assistance has risen from 1.5 million to over 3 million.

22 See K. Sontheimer / H. Röhring, *Handbuch des politischen Systems der Bundesrepublik Deutschland*, Munich 1977, pp. 621 ff.

23 This is particularly true of the *Gymnasien* (grammar or high schools). *Realschulen* (intermediate-grade secondary schools) and *Hauptschulen* (lower-grade secondary schools), on the other hand, teach practical techniques that can be used in later working life.

24 Inter-company training centres are normally established and maintained by chambers of industry and commerce and chambers of the crafts with government assistance.

25 According to the findings of a World Bank study, countries with an independent central bank are generally more successful in combating inflation than countries with a dependent central bank. However, there are exceptions. Such countries as Japan and Singapore have proved as successful as Germany in combating inflation even though their central banks operate to instructions from their governments. World Bank, *Policy Research Bulletin,* Vol. 3, 1992, No. 5, p. 2.

26 The structural inequality of supply and demand in the labour market is a result of the different elasticities. Unlike the employer, the individual employee cannot "wait": he must offer his labour. His bargaining position is thus bound to be weaker than the employer's. Closely linked to this is his atypical supply reaction. He does not reduce the supply of labour when wages fall as a result of an excess of supply over demand. Instead, he tries to counteract the reduction in the income from labour he needs by increasing his labour input. Furthermore, the cost of adjustment appropriate to the market (change of location or occupation) is too high for the market mechanism to be able to function without friction at all times.

27 In this respect the Collective Agreements Act is comparable to the *Bundesbank* Act. The independence of the *Bundesbank* could also be waived by a simple majority in the *Bundestag.* Yet its independence is regarded as "inviolable".

28 This does not apply to collective bargaining in the public sector, where the state is the employer and thus a party to the collective bargaining.

29 Besides the unions belonging to the Federation of German Trade Unions, there are a number of others, but they are not, on the whole, of any major significance.

30 The various sectors are also broken down into regions. There are, in all, 3,000 sectoral/regional areas and the same number of wage settlements.

31 There are different arrangements for specific groups of people, e.g. seasonal workers and young people.

32 It is not always easy to draw a line between employee participation in a plant and employee participation in an enterprise. In principle, it depends on the entity's purpose: a plant's goal is of a technical nature, while an enterprise pursues an economic objective.

36 The income threshold for health insurance in 1993 was DM 5,400 per month.

37 After this period the employee receives welfare benefit.

38 *Federal Ministry of Employment and Social Affairs, Übersicht,* op. cit., p. 72.

39 With the total population declining, the trend in the ratio of young people (up to the age of 20) to the gainfully employed (20 to 60) is slightly downward, while the ratio of the over-60s to the working population will become far worse, rising from 36% in 1990 to 77% in the year 2030 (all figures relate to the old *Länder*). This trend will strike at the very heart of the principle of solidarity, which in pension insurance is reflected in the compact among the generations and in statutory health insurance in contributions that depend entirely on income. While there was one pensioner for every two contributors in the mid-1980s, a statistical average of one pensioner will have to be financed by one contributor in 2030. In health insurance the growing proportion of elderly people alone is likely to lead to an explosive rise in costs, which will encourage the younger generation to turn away from the idea of solidarity and new forms of insurance for specific groups to emerge.

40 K. Izawa, *Japan und die Weltzivilisation,* in: R. Schwarz (ed.), *Menschliche Existenz und moderne Welt,* Part II, Berlin 1967, p. 322.

41 M. Miegel, op. cit., p. 42.

42 Ibid., p. 41.

43 The recommendations made by an adviser on economic policy will, for example, usually be based on the market economy system he knows best, i.e. his own country's.

www.ingramcontent.com/pod-product-compliance
Ingram Content Group UK Ltd.
Pitfield, Milton Keynes, MK11 3LW, UK
UKHW041839280225
455677UK00010B/257